Auntie,
I wish we were going to
Of flipping through these pages! Merry Christmas! I love you
very much!
Love,
Daniel

MW01399917

# My Italy in Pictures

©Ivet Graham-Morgan. All rights reserved. No part of this publication may be reproduced or transmitted in any form or by any means, electronic or mechanical, including photocopying, recording, or by any information storage and retrieval system, without the written permission of the author.

Dedication – To Travellers Everywhere

Italy, an extremely beautiful country, is home to the greatest number of UNESCO World Heritage Sites. The country boasts several world-famous cities such as Rome, Florence, Turin, Milan, and Venice. It is estimated that Italy is home to half the world's great art treasures. Italy has an impressive collection of archaeological sites, churches, monasteries, assorted castles, towers and fortresses, stately homes, gardens, major historic town centres and much more.

Italy has been home to many distinguished and influential civilizations, including the Etruscans, Greeks, and the Romans. Dating back to ancient times until the mid-17th century, Italy was respected as the central place of Western culture and the starting point of worldwide trends. Italy is the place where a number of famous painters, sculptors, poets, musicians, mathematicians and architects developed and launched their career and eventually carved a place of their own in history.

Located on the Italian Peninsula, Italy is the most southern European nation. It is surrounded in the north by Austria, France, Switzerland, and Slovenia. Italy shares the Italian Peninsula with Vatican City and San Marino which are independent territories within the same geographical region.

The Italian territory includes the southern side of the Alps, the large plain of Po Valley and the islands of Sardinia and Sicily as well as the Tuscan island chain. Italy has a vast coastline that extends all the way to the Adriatic Sea, Ionian Sea, Tyrrhenian Sea, Ligurian Sea, Sea of Sardinia, and the Strait of Sicily. Influenced by locations, Italy enjoys a variety of climate systems – including tundra climate, cold continental climate, humid continental climate, oceanic climate, humid subtropical climate, Mediterranean mild climate, Mediterranean climate, as well as extremes.

Italy is largely a mountainous country—with the Apennine Mountains forming the backbone of the peninsula and the Alps as the northern boundary. Nestled between these two mountain ranges is the Po Valley which is the largest plain in Italy and embodies more than 70% of the total plain area in the country.

Some components of the Italian territory are of volcanic origin. Most of the small islands and archipelagos in the south are volcanic islands. Etna the largest active volcano in Europe is in Sicily, and then there is volcano Stromboli and Vesuvius near Naples.

I can think of no better way to convey the beauty of Italy than with pictures. The old adage, "A picture is worth a thousand words" is perhaps, an overused catchphrase but in this case that familiar old adage is a perfect fit.

It is my hope that readers will have as much pleasure leafing through the pages of this book as I have had putting it together.

**Aosta Valley, Italy** - The beautiful Aosta Valley in all its glory… Its natural beauty and peaceful ambiance keep tourism strong in the region.

**Lazio, Italy** – A region rich in archaeology and charming landscape
Sunset settles over the pictorial landscape of the Lazio region ushering in its magical charm.

**Aosta Valley, Italy** – Another Picturesque view of the region The Aosta Valley is made up of several valleys including the Aosta Valley from which the region took its name. The landscape is characterized by glaciers, lakes, nature parks, grasslands, forests, and villages.

A view of the Aosta Valley with soft, mountain peaks in the backdrop

A mountain stream meanders through the gorgeous Aosta Valley

Another scenic view of the Aosta Valley - The region offers amazing natural attractions.

Rome, Italy – Interior of the famous Saint Peter's Basilica

Considered the most important temple for the Catholic Church

One of the many alluring waterfalls dotting the Italian Landscape

Syracuse Dome on the island of Sicily, Italy

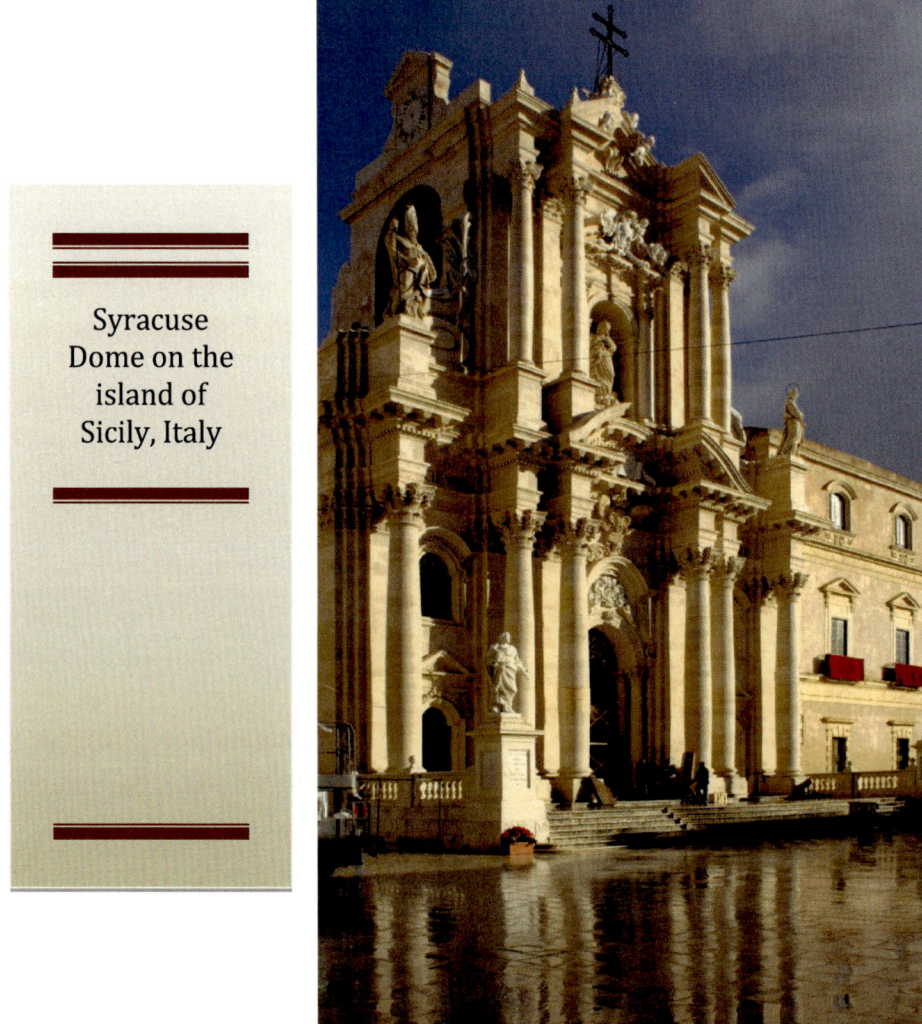

**Padova,** a city in northern Italy, it stands on the Bacchiglione River about 25 miles west of Venice and is sometimes included with Venice.

**Sesto Calende -** Located at the southern tip of Lake Maggiore in the Lombardy region of northern Italy, it lies in the vicinity where the Ticino River starts flowing towards the Po River. The Abbey of San Donato, a 9th - 10th century structure housing a painting by Bernardino Zenale is the foremost historical attraction here.

**Verbania** – Lies on the shore of lovely Lake Maggiore, a large lake located on the south side of the Alps and shared between Italy and Switzerland. Verbania is 25 miles from Locarno in Switzerland and approximately 57 miles from Milan.

**Verbania -** On the shore of Lake Maggiore accentuated by towering mountains reaching for the sky

**Amalfi Coast of Italy** – These rock formations are known as the Faraglioni and consist of three distinct formations that have been named. To the left is Faraglione di Fuori A.K.A. Scopolo which is habitat to the Italian wall lizard, podarcis siculus. Next is Faraglione di Mezzo branded by a hollow that forms a natural tunnel through which small boats can sail. Next is Stella which is not visible in this picture - Stella is still attached to the coast.

**Amalfi Coast** – Located in southern Italy, the beautiful Amalfi coast surrounded by dramatic cliffs has long been a playground for the wealth. In the 1920s and 1930s it was a popular holiday place for British upper class and aristocracy. Today, the Amalfi coast is still a sought-after destination; although, it is a bit on the pricey side.

**Tuscany, Italy** – A region known for the artistic masterpieces of her cities and the beauty of her natural landscape.

## Venice, Italy

Canals serve as the main conduits of the city – for most visitors to the city the major appeal lies in its many canals.

**Castellina in Chianti,** A township of Etruscan and Roman origin, in the Tuscany region of Italy, it forms a part of the Chianti Hills between the valleys of the Arbia, Pesa and Elsa rivers.

**Tuscany** - Historic homes dating back to the Middle Ages. A region known for its history and artistic legacy, it is seen as the home of Italian Renaissance. Along with her capital Florence, the Tuscany region is a trendy tourist destination.

**Tivoli** – lies in Lazio, Italy and is about 19 miles from Rome. Formerly the ancient city of Tibur, abounding with water streams and lush countryside, it became a resort to the wealthy of the day. Emperor Hadrian built a villa here.

**Doge's Palace** – Built in Venetian Gothic style, the palace was the residence of the Dodge of Venice when Venice was a Republic. The highest authority of the Republic of Venice, the office was an elected one and was a position held for life. Today, the palace is one of the major landmarks of the city of Venice.

**Venice City, Italy**

These are the traditional flat-bottomed Venetian rowing boat known as gondola. They are considered suitable for the conditions of the Venetian lagoon.

**Torre del Mangia**

A medieval tower in Siena, Tuscany

**Sicily, Italy**

**Cefalu** located on the northern coast of Sicily on the Tyrrhenian Sea is a major tourist attraction.

**River Arno in Pisa** – Tuscany region of Italy - after the Tiber River, the Arno River is one of the most important rivers in Central Italy.

**City of Florence** on the Arno River

The **Ponte Vecchio -** A medieval bridge over the Arno River in Florence, that spans the Arno at its narrowest point. It is a closed bridge that has more than one floors and has shops along it, as was common in the period.

The **Ponte Santa Trinita** – oldest elliptic arch bridge in the world - stretches over the Arno River in Florence, Italy.

The ancient city of **Florence, Italy** gained respect as one of the most important cities of Europe and the world from as far back as the 14th century. Today, Florence is still highly respected and does enjoy her fair share of the tourist industry every year.

Close-up shot of **Syracuse Dome** on the island of Sicily, Italy

**Caltagirone, Sicily, Italy –**

This is the 142-step historic monument of Santa Maria del Monte, built in 1608.

Each step is decorated with different hand-decorated ceramic using styles and figures from ancient pottery-making in the region.

The **Villnober Bach** – A mountain stream in South Tyrol, Italy

**Venice** is legendary for the splendour of its setting

**Venice** is well known not only for the splendour of its setting but also for its architecture, and artwork.

Beautiful **Venice**, a city separated by canals and linked by bridges.

**Venice city** shrouded in all her stateliness sits contentedly in the beautiful Venetian Lagoon.

**Venice, Italy** – A show of beautiful architecture and a stark reminder of those that engineered this innovative community.

Gondolas navigate the turquoise water shimmering between grand old buildings perched on the gorgeous Venetian Lagoon.

This is **Piazza San Marco** the major public square of Venice, Italy.

Modica, an ancient city in Sicily believed to have been established either in 1031 BC or 1360 BC.

Partial view of Duomo di San Giorgio in Ragusa Sicily, Italy

Partial view of the interior of **Piazza San Marco** the major public square of Venice, Italy

**Pisa, Italy -** This is the Arno River, a river in the Tuscany region of Italy. It is one of central Italy's most important rivers.

Venice, Italy – The **Grand Canal** forms one of the main water-traffic corridors in the city. Public transportation is by water buses and private water taxis. Most tourist sightsee the canal by gondola, a traditional flat-bottomed Venetian rowing boat.

**Rialto Bridge** – One of four bridges crossing the Grand Canal in Venice, Italy and the oldest bridge across the canal

**Tiber River** – Third longest river in Italy, with Saint Peter's Basilica in the distance

Rome, Italy – **Ponte Sant' Angelo**, a bridge built by Roman Emperor Hadrian across the Tiber River. It was completed in 134 AD. In ancient times pilgrims used this bridge to get to get to St. Peter's Basilica.

Rome, Italy - **St. Peter's and the Vatican** viewed from Castel Sant' Angelo, a fortress, which was built in AD 130 -139 as a mausoleum for Emperor Hadrian.

Rome, Italy – St. Peter's Basilica in St. Peter's Square

Sicily, Italy – **Ragusa,** a city on the island of Sicily built on a limestone hill between two deep valleys.

**Tirano, Italy** - A scenic town located in northern Italy, near to the border between Italy and Switzerland.

**Venice, Italy** – Beautiful architecture compliments the ambience lurking in this magical place.

**Venice, Italy –** Another scenic view of the Grand Canal

**Venice, Italy** – Gondolas skim the lagoon unhurriedly - great place for a delightful holiday.

**Venice, Italy** – Cruising the emerald waters of the Venetian Lagoon

**Venice, Italy –** Another enchanting view of fine architectural structures in the Venetian Lagoon.

Venice, Italy - This is the island of **San Michele**. It is on this island that the cemetery is located since burial on the main islands in the Venetian lagoon is considered unsanitary.

**Venice** - Beautiful display of row houses and a connecting bridge stretching across the canal.

This is Burano, one of the 118 islands that make up Venice. This area is known for its colorful houses and lacework.

Venice, Italy – the Grand Canal

**Grado, Italy** - A town nestled on a peninsula of the Adriatic Sea between Venice and Trieste. A popular tourist destination, Grado lies in the impressive natural setting of the Grado lagoon.

**Isola San Giulio -** an island in north western Italy surrounded by Lake Orta. The most prominent building on the island is the Basilicia of Saint Giulio.

**Lake Garda** – Located in northern Italy, beautiful Lake Garda is Italy's largest lake and a very popular tourist destination.

**Molveno Lake, Italy** – Located on the Italian Alps, Molveno, a well-known tourist destination overlooks the beautiful Lake Molveno, surrounded by the charming Brenta Dolomites mountain range. The area is ideal for nature lovers – one can enjoy long walks along the banks of the lake or a relaxing boat ride on her inviting surface.

**Trieste City –** Lies on the Gulf of Trieste in northeast Italy near the border with Slovenia.

A spectacular view of the lovely Amalfi coast, Italy – a holiday paradise

Sicily, Italy - The **Cyclopean Isles** are of volcanic origin and lie off the eastern coast of Sicily in the Mediterranean Sea near to Mount Etna. Noted for the rows of basaltic columns piled one above another, they closely resemble the Giant's Causeway on the northern coast of Ireland.

**Tindari** in Sicily, Italy – Famous for the statue of the black Madonna and a black Baby Jesus

Sicily, Italy – Interior of **Taormina Giardini Naxos** Railway Station

**Hermitage of Santa Caterina del Sasso -** Perched on a rocky ridge on the eastern shore of Lake Maggiore in the Lombardy region, this Roman Catholic monastery can be reached by boat, elevator, or by taking a long winding stairway.

**Catania,** Sicily – Cruise ship in the bay

**Catania, Sicily –** Under clear skies, a beautiful cloud hovers over the bay

Amidst lush, emerald vegetation **Lake Garda** relaxes against the back drop of towering rocks.

A panoramic view that simply locks in the charm and grandeur of the striking Italian landscape

**Sicily, Italy** – Plant life thrive in the rich lava deposit from Mount Etna

**Sicily, Italy** – A flowering plant that thrives on Mount Etna

**Cefalu** – A major tourist attraction on the Tyrrhenian Sea, it lies on the northern coast of Sicily, Italy.

The iconic tower of Pisa is a bell tower renowned for its vivid tilt to one side. It is the third oldest building in the Cathedral Square at Pisa.

Precise preparation is essential for every trans-alps tour - taking into consideration Physical needs and the condition of the mountain bike to be used for the tour. A trans-alps tour takes an average of four to six days covering about 90 km per day and crossing at various altitudes. The nights are spent in inns and guest houses along the way.

The best time for crossing the Alps is during the summer months when there is no snow or just a little snow on mountain tops. Those who dare to cross are rewarded with the scenic view that can only be realized from an elevation of this magnitude.

This is Stromboli, a small volcanic island in the Tyrrhenian Sea off the coast of north Sicily. It is one of the three active volcanoes in Italy.

**Mount Stromboli**, nicknamed Lighthouse of the Mediterranean, is constantly active with minor eruptions – it is virtually erupting continuously and has been doing so for about 2000 years.

**Sicily, Italy** - Hot volcanic steam

**Sicily, Italy** – Interestingly shaped volcanic rock

**Mount Etna** in Sicily, Italy

Cloud of smoke as Mount Etna erupted in 2002 – Mount Etna is the highest mountain in Italy south of the Alps and the largest of the three active volcanoes in Italy – Etna is a very popular tourist attraction.

**Mount Etna** volcanic eruption in 2002 – Labelled a *Decade Volcano* by the United Nations because of its history of eruption and the population living in nearby areas – Mount Etna has recently been added to the UNESCO World Heritage Sites.

**Tuscany, Italy** - A beautiful sunrise over the sleepy mountains - An area well known for its alluring landscapes, Tuscany has a western coastline on the Tyrrhenian Sea that contains the Tuscan Archipelago including the island of Elba which is the largest stretch of land from the ancient tract once connecting the Italian peninsula to Corsica.

The Three Peaks of Lavaredo (Tre Cime di Lavaredo) - north wall pinnacle view. This is perhaps one of the most well-known mountain groups in the Alps. These peaks once marked the boundary between Austria and Italy. Today, these peaks lie between the Italian provinces of Belluno and South Tyrol with the Italian-speaking majority on one side and the German-speaking on the other.

Lake Misurina in the Italian Alps flanked by lovely evergreen and mountain peaks towering in the background

**South Tyrol, Italy** – A breath-taking view of the Dolomite Mountains stretched against blue sky accented by pockets of fluffy clouds

**South Tyrol, Italy** - snow-capped Mountains against a partially blue sky

**South Tyrol** – Given the remarkable landscape, South Tyrol is a popular spot for hikers. There are marked hiking and mountain trails which create opportunities to explore from the valley floor to the highest peaks.

**Hiking the Dolomites** of northern Italy is a real treat. It can be enjoyed simply by taking a leisurely stroll along scenic trails or by taking an adventurous trek across the wild alpine meadows, lakes and soaring mountain peaks.

**Dolomite Mountains** – Popular with hikers, it features countless numbers of trails that wind their way through incredible landscapes with awe-inspiring views. There are trails suitable for every interest and aptitude level – anything from day trips to long treks.

**Sibillini Mountains** – Nestled between eastern Umbria and the Marche, they are a mountain group in Italy that is part of the central Apennines - composed mainly of limestone rocks.

A perfect shot of the Dolomites, a mountain range located in northeastern Italy, as it towers against the expanse of the vivid blue sky.

Towering peaks of the Dolomites mountain range framed against the Italian sky

**Haflinger** or **Avelignese** - Known for endurance, this breed was developed to work in mountainous terrain. The breed was developed in northern Italy and Austria in the late 19th century – Cross breed between the Arabian horse and several European breeds.

**Villa Borghese Gardens** – Third largest public garden in Rome – it contains several buildings, museums, and attractions.

Made in the USA
Lexington, KY
15 December 2017